DISCOVERING CANADA

The Mounties

ROBERT LIVESEY & A.G. SMITH

Fitzhenry & Whiteside

Published in Canada by Fitzhenry & Whiteside, 195 Allstate Parkway, Markham, Ontario L3R 4T8

Published in the United States by Fitzhenry & Whiteside, 311 Washington Street, Brighton, Massachusetts 02135

www.fitzhenry.ca   godwit@fitzhenry.ca

10   9   8   7   6   5   4   3   2   1

Library and Archives Canada Cataloguing in Publication
Livesey, Robert, 1940-
      The Mounties / Robert Livesey ; illustrated by A.G. Smith.
(Discovering Canada)
Includes index.
ISBN 978-1-55005-135-3
      1. Royal Canadian Mounted Police—History—Juvenile literature.
      I. Smith, A. G. (Albert Gray), 1945- II. Title. III. Series.
      Livesey, Robert, 1940- . Discovering Canada.

FC3216.2.L59 2008   j363.20971   C2007-907007-8

Fitzhenry & Whiteside acknowledges with thanks the Canada Council for the Arts, and the Ontario Arts Council for their support of our publishing program. We acknowledge the financial support of the Government of Canada through the Book Publishing Industry Development Program (BPIDP) for our publishing activities.

Canada Council   Conseil des Arts   ONTARIO ARTS COUNCIL
for the Arts   du Canada   CONSEIL DES ARTS DE L'ONTARIO

Illustrations by A.G. Smith
Cover and interior by Janie Skeete, Skeedoodle Design

Printed in Canada

Dedicated to cousins
Elizabeth, Kimberly, Jennifer, Wendy, Jessica,
and Susan.

A special thanks to Sophie C. Forget, Historian, and Daniel Somers,
Historian, RCMP Historical Section; Josie Hazen; Linda Biesenthal;
Kathy Vanderlinden; Janie Skeete; Christina Kim; John and Marci Burn;
and the librarians at the Hamilton Public Library
and the University of Windsor Library.

Books in the Discovering Canada series:

Contents

Introduction

John A. Macdonald was Canada's first prime minister when the Dominion of Canada was formed in 1867. He joined together the British colonies of Upper Canada (Ontario), Lower Canada (Quebec), Nova Scotia, and New Brunswick.

In 1869, Macdonald purchased Rupert's Land, the vast northern trading territories of the Hudson's Bay Company, which had been established in 1670.

Rupert's Land became part of Canada's Northwest Territories, which was officially created on July 15, 1870. It extended north to the Arctic Ocean and stretched west from the new Canadian province of Manitoba on the Red River to the colony of British Columbia on the Pacific Ocean.

Macdonald moved fast to protect Canada's new territory. The United States had developed communities on its western prairies and the California coast. American fur traders had pushed north to occupy the Canadian lands, which were populated by buffalo hunters and Native people. The Americans brought cheap liquor to trade for furs. They built secure strongholds, forts with dramatic names such as Fort Slide Out and Fort Standoff. The wildest and most infamous of the whisky trading camps was Fort Whoop-Up.

South of the border, the "wild west" depicted later in Hollywood movies had been overrun by intruders so quickly that it led to bands of outlaws, lawless frontier towns, and bloody battles with the Native people.

Macdonald was aware of the ruthless American expansion and the violence it created. There was no established order in the "wild west." The new

American towns elected or appointed sheriffs who made their own laws. A stranger had to learn quickly the unique rules of the community because he or she could be shot or hanged for breaking them. Native people were not protected by these laws, and their ancient traditions were ignored by the swarm of settlers invading the American west.

Macdonald was determined to establish a safe, orderly Canadian west, where the same laws applied to both new settlers and Native people. In 1873, he learned that American whisky traders, known as the Hardwick Gang, had massacred a group of Assiniboines in the Cypress Hills. Macdonald appointed a lieutenant governor and council to run the new territory. Then he created a federal military police force to guard and protect it. The new force, mounted on horseback, policed the territory and applied one justice system equally to everyone. The North-West Mounted Police in their bright red uniforms became the crimson justice on the Canadian prairies.

Mountie Motto

Hollywood movies, television, books, and other entertainment media have created the myth that the Mounties always "get their man." The real motto of the force is *Maintiens le droit*, or Defending the Law.

Scarlet Uniforms

Prime Minister John A. Macdonald personally designed the red uniform of the Mounties. It was based on the uniform of the Royal Irish Constabulary, a police force famous in the British Empire for establishing order against protesters and rebels. Macdonald also used the blue-coated mounted cavalry of the American army as a military model for the new force.

Whoop-Up Bug Juice

Before the arrival of the Mounties in 1874, American whisky traders ruled the foothills of the Rocky Mountains. Fort Whoop-Up was operated by Alfred B. Hamilton and his followers. They flew their own flag, which was similar to the American flag but without stars. They corrupted the Native people with their own brew of liquor known as Whoop-Up bug juice.

Intoxicated with bug juice, the Native people had burned the Hudson's Bay Company forts on the Bow and Red Deer rivers. The legitimate fur traders were forced from the area in fear of being robbed or killed.

1 *Scarlet Soldiers*

George French, James Macleod, Jerry Potts, and Others

The North-West Mounted Police,* also known as the NWMP or Mounties, was created by an act of the Canadian Parliament on May 23, 1873, then officially established by an Order-in-Council on August 30, 1873. That allowed recruiting to start.

The commanding officer of the Mounties was called the commissioner. The first permanent commissioner was George A. French.

Three hundred men between the ages of 18 and 40 were selected to serve in the paramilitary force. Each recruit was tall and strong, of good character, in good health, able to read and write in either English or French, and trained to ride a horse. Sub-constables were paid 75 cents a day; constables received $1.00 a day. They gathered at the settlement of Fort Dufferin in Manitoba and were divided into six troops of 50 men each.

The Long March West

On July 8, 1874, Commissioner French led the Mounties on a 1200-km march west to the junction of the Bow and Belly rivers (in southern Alberta today). His objective was to locate and shut down Fort Whoop-Up, the stronghold of the illegal whisky traders. For two months, the parade of 67 covered wagons, 114 ox carts, 90 cattle, 310 horses, farming equipment, and artillery guns snaked its way across the prairies.

* In 1873, the original name was the Mounted Police Force of the North-West Territories. In 1879, it officially became the North-West Mounted Police.

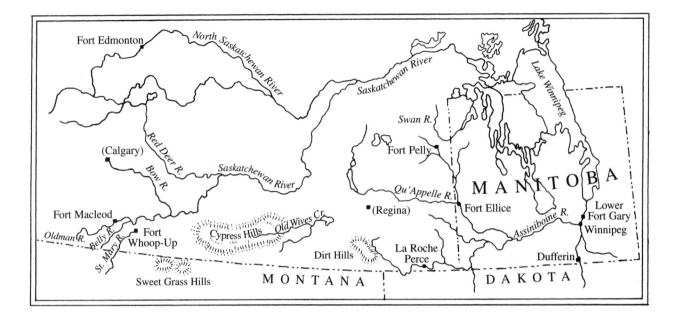

The cavalcade of red-coated troops was bitten by black-flies, scorched by the hot sun, and torn by tornadoes. Wagons broke down or were bogged down in deep mud as they proceeded over steep hills and across wide rivers. The horses were thin from starvation; the men were exhausted. They found themselves lost on the endless flat prairie. George French wrote in his diary that he was "alarmed for the safety of the Force."

Finally, they reached La Roche Perce. There the force split up; a troop headed northwest to Fort Edmonton, a Hudson's Bay Company post. The rest struggled west to the Sweet Grass Hills near the American border.

Commissioner George French and his assistant commissioner, James F. Macleod, took a small party of men to obtain food and new horses from Fort Benton in Montana. French then took troops D and E to Swan River, the designated headquarters of the new police force. Macleod proceeded west with B, C, and F troops into the foothills in search of Fort Whoop-Up.

6

George French

George Arthur French, an Irishman and the force's first commissioner, was a tall, 32-year-old artillery officer. He had previously been the commandant of the School of Gunnery at Kingston, Ontario.

Commissioner French led the long march across the prairies in 1874. His skills in navigation and his knowledge of the stars, the sun, and the pole star ensured that the weary band of police officers arrived safely in the Sweet Grass Hills.

When he finally reached Blackfoot territory, George French encountered a respected Blackfoot warrior, Bear Child. Bear Child's original name was Jerry Potts. He was a Métis whose father had been a Scottish trader. Commissioner French hired Jerry Potts as a scout and interpreter.

Bull's Head

The Native people called Assistant Commissioner James Macleod *Stamixotoken*, which means Bull's Head. He was a 38-year-old, Scottish-born adventurer who had been educated as a lawyer in Upper Canada. When Macleod first encountered a herd of buffalo, he was intrigued by the size and nobility of the awesome animals. His recommendation that their image be placed on the buttons of the Mountie uniforms was approved. Later he hung a buffalo head over his office door at Fort Macleod.

Finding Fort Whoop-Up

Before the Mounties arrived on the lawless Canadian frontier, it was populated by Native people and unscrupulous whisky traders, such as those at Fort Whoop-Up. The traders exchanged illegal alcohol and guns for buffalo robes supplied by the Native hunters.

The job of the new police force was to establish law and order. James Macleod, with Jerry Potts as a guide, went in search of Fort Whoop-Up. On October 9, 1874, the column of scarlet soldiers arrived at the junction of the Belly and St. Mary rivers. Jerry Potts pointed at Fort Whoop-Up. Then Macleod and Potts rode up to the stockade, entered, and found it empty, except for a fur trader and a few Native people. The illegal whisky traders had fled south across the U.S. border when they were warned that the large force of red-coated, mounted police officers was approaching.

James Macleod's orders were to build a police fort in the wilderness. Jerry Potts led him another 45 km to a broad loop of the Oldman River in the heart of Blackfoot territory. There the Mounties constructed Fort Macleod. Other police forts, Fort Saskatchewan, Fort Calgary, and Fort Walsh, were built by 1875. Law and order had arrived in Canada's Northwest Territories.

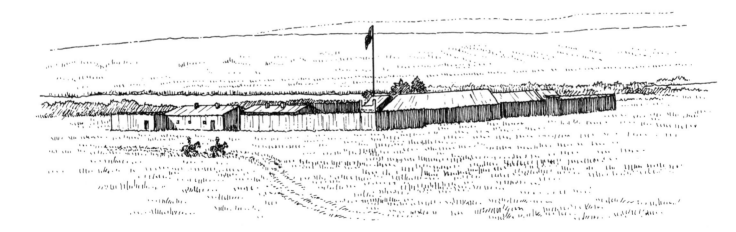

Bear Child*

Sixteen-year-old Jerry Potts leaned casually against a counter inside the Fort Benton trading post in Montana. His father, Andrew Potts, a Scottish fur trader, was upstairs closing the shutters on the windows against the cold of a prairie night. Andrew had earned a reputation as a fair dealer among both white and Native people at a time when few traders had such respect. Jerry's mother, Crooked Back, belonged to the Black Elk Band of the Blood First Nation.

Suddenly, Jerry's head jerked upwards at the sharp crack of a rifle. In the same instant, he heard his father's body crash through an upper window and then hit the ground with a heavy thud. As the boy rushed outside and fell on his knees beside his dead parent, he caught sight of a Blackfoot warrior on a pony disappearing into the northern dusk.

Jerry knew instantly what had happened and rushed to saddle his horse. Earlier that day, the Blackfoot had tried to obtain credit and had argued with an employee of the fur company. To ease the situation, Mr. Potts had sent the clerk away on an errand, and thus was closing the windows himself. Thinking the figure on the second floor was the employee, the Blackfoot warrior had shot Jerry's father in error.

Young Jerry doggedly followed the trail of the murderer both day and night until, far to the north on the Canadian prairies, he finally caught up to him in the middle of a Blackfoot camp. Ignoring personal danger, Jerry attacked and stabbed his father's killer. Bravery was a high-ranking virtue in the Blackfoot code. Young Jerry had added boldness, resourcefulness, and courage to the good name he already possessed by being his father's son. From that moment, he was welcomed into all Blackfoot camps and, among other honours, was invited to join the inner council of the proud Blackfoot Confederacy. He never

* Jerry Potts was a legendary personality. There are other versions of the story of his boyhood and how he became a Blackfoot warrior.

returned to the empty trading post, choosing instead to live the free life of a Blackfoot. He was given the name *Ky-yo-kosi*, which means Bear Child.

Legendary Scout

The main reason that the Blackfoot accepted the Mounties was Jerry Potts. He assured the Blackfoot that the scarlet-coated police officers would bring equal justice for Native people and white settlers or traders.

Jerry Potts continued working as a scout for the Mounties for 22 years and became a western legend. In 1877, he acted as interpreter at the signing of Treaty No. 7 at Blackfoot Crossing. His participation guaranteed that the Mounties and the Blackfoot came to a peaceful agreement.

Jerry Potts was an unforgettable personality. It was said that the short, slope-shouldered plainsman could smell water eight kilometres away and that his legs were moulded to his saddle. He wore the skin of a wild cat under his shirt because he had experienced a vision during a dream that it would protect him. Jerry was a man of few words. Once, when he was asked what was beyond the next hill, he replied tersely, "Another hill." On another occasion, after a Native chief had spoken to the white authorities for 90 minutes, Jerry interpreted the speech simply by saying, "He wants grub." Jerry could navigate the vast plains without losing his way; one Mountie suggested that he must have "a compass in his gizzard."

When Jerry Potts died in 1896 at the age of 61 from cancer of the throat, he was buried at Fort Macleod with full military honours.

First Arrest

The first desperadoes arrested by the Mounties were five illegal whisky traders led by William Bond. When a Native chief named Three Bulls informed James Macleod that the whisky traders were operating in the area, Macleod ordered Inspector N.L.F. "Paddy" Crozier to capture them.

Paddy Crozier chose his 10 best officers and horses. Accompanied by Jerry Potts, they left Fort Macleod in pursuit of the culprits. Jerry tracked the traders, and when the Mounties caught up with them, Crozier demanded: "Halt! In the name of the Queen!"

The captured traders were escorted back to Fort Macleod. James Macleod tried them and found them guilty. He confiscated their whisky, guns, and 116 buffalo robes. But there was no jail at Fort Macleod, and William Bond managed to escape in the night. In the spring after the snow had melted, Bond's frozen corpse was discovered.

Powwow with Crowfoot

The powerful Chief Crowfoot of the Blackfoot First Nation, wearing a deer-skin jacket decorated with black symbols that represented his battle victories, came to Fort Macleod to meet with James Macleod, who was already famous as Bull's Head. Crowfoot was so impressed by the red-jacketed Mountie that he returned a few days later with all the chiefs of the Blackfoot, Blood, and Peigan nations for a powwow. Jerry Potts acted as interpreter.

After the peace pipe was lit with a buffalo chip, it was passed around the group. Then Macleod announced: "I come from the Great White Queen. I come in friendship." He explained that he would not steal land from the Native people. Instead, he would negotiate and buy or trade for any lands that he required. When the powwow was over, Macleod had become a friend and the wise Chief Crowfoot encouraged him to end the whisky trade.

The Hardwick Gang

James Macleod had many challenges as the commander of Fort Macleod. Because there was no money to pay his men, no fresh uniforms, and no mail from the east, 18 of his troops deserted. But one of his greatest challenges was trying to capture the infamous Hardwick Gang.

The Hardwick Gang, who had murdered the Assiniboines in the Cypress Hills in 1873, were from the "wild west" town of Helena, Montana. Macleod's orders were to travel to Montana, arrest the gang, and bring the men back to Canada to stand trial. He sent an undercover agent, A.G. Irvine, to Helena to gather evidence and find witnesses. Irvine had been an army lieutenant-colonel and commandant of the Red River garrison before he became a police inspector and was sent on the secret assignment.

The 50-km trip south to Helena involved crossing the deadly Badlands.

Guided by Jerry Potts, Macleod and three other Mounties set out to cross the dangerous terrain, but got caught in a winter blizzard. Jerry had the uncanny ability to find his way in the dead of night or in severe snowstorms. In temperatures of 55 degrees below zero, the Mounties stumbled after Potts, who found refuge from the elements in a ravine. Using hunting knives to dig a cave in the snowbanks, they huddled there for 36 hours. Macleod's face froze; one Mountie went snow-blind and froze his foot.

When Macleod reached Helena, he arrested and charged 14 men with murder. But the American judge refused to extradite them to Canada. The men in the Hardwick Gang were local heroes, and menacing mobs of frontiersmen confronted the Mounties. Macleod was arrested, but was soon released and forced to return without his prisoners.

In May 1875, Jerry Potts guided Inspector J.M. Walsh and B Division across 260 km east into the Cypress Hills. There they established Fort Walsh at the site where the Assiniboines had been massacred.

Treaty No. 6

By spring 1876, the U.S. Army was in a hostile conflict over territory with the American Sioux. In contrast, the Canadian government was peacefully negotiating with the Saskatchewan First Nations and the Blackfoot Confederacy to obtain land titles. When Treaty No. 6 was signed by the Cree and the Assiniboine nations in 1876, the Native people gave up their title to 310,000 km^2 in present-day central Saskatchewan and Alberta.

Treaty No. 7

In 1877, James Macleod replaced George French and became the second commissioner of the police force. In September, Macleod and the lieutenant governor of the Northwest Territories, David Laird, met with the chiefs of the Blackfoot Confederacy at Blackfoot Crossing. Because Macleod had previously won the trust of the most powerful Native chiefs – Crowfoot, Old Sun, and Red Crow – the Blackfoot Confederacy signed Treaty No. 7, giving up the title to what is today southern Alberta. It allowed for the building of the transcontinental railway and the peaceful settlement of the Canadian west.

Macleod and Laird were escorted by 50 Mounties on horseback in bright crimson uniforms and greeted by the police band. Each of the chiefs of the Blackfoot, Blood, Peigan, Sarcee, and other First Nations made his mark on the treaty. About 4000 Native men, women, and children watched. Mrs. Macleod, the wives of the other officers, priests, missionaries, and settlers also signed as witnesses. The ceremony ended with a 13-gun salute.

Praise from Crowfoot

When Chief Crowfoot signed Treaty No. 7, also known as the Blackfoot Treaty, he acknowledged the good advice and protection offered by the Mounties. He stated: "If the police had not come to this country, where would we all be now? Bad men and whisky were killing us so fast that very few of us would have been left today. The Mounted Police have protected us as the feathers of the bird protect it from the frosts of winter."

Newspaper Artist

The long trek west by Commissioner French with 300 Mounties was recorded by Henri Julien, a journalist and artist for a Montreal periodical called the *Canadian Illustrated News*.

In November 1879, a young Mountie named Marmaduke Graburn had a confrontation at Fort Walsh with Star Child, a member of the Blood Nation. Later that day, when Graburn did not return from an errand, patrols were sent out to find him, but without success. Jerry Potts found the trail and eventually the Mountie's body. He had been shot in the back. Star Child fled south across the border, but a year later returned to his Blood camp.

Corporal Patterson and three other Mounties were led to the camp by Jerry Potts. When confronted, Star Child fired his rifle, which brought the rest of the camp to his rescue. Patterson grabbed the culprit off his feet, and the Mounties galloped the 40 km to Fort Walsh, chased by Blood warriors. A jury later found Star Child innocent because of lack of evidence.

*Mountie Stock
Saddle*

Make a Mountie Pillbox Cap

The original Mountie uniform included a blue and gold pillbox cap. It was worn tilted to one side of the head with a cord under the chin.

What you need:

- scissors
- ruler
- pencil
- white glue
- scoring tool
- shoelace
- yellow bond paper
- dark blue construction paper

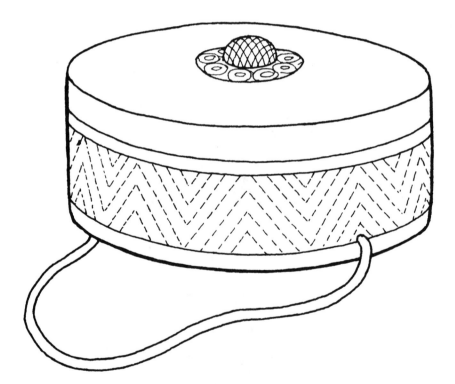

16

What to do:

1. Using a large sheet of blue construction paper, copy the pattern for the rectangle and the circle as shown in the diagram on page 18.
2. Apply glue to the tab of the rectangle and attach it to the opposite side to form a cylinder. Leave to dry.
3. Lightly score the tabs around the edge of the circle and fold the tabs up. Carefully push the circle down into the cylinder. Glue the tabs to the side of the cylinder.
4. On yellow bond paper, make four photocopies of the braided band on page 19. Cut out and glue all the way around the bottom of the cap.
5. Make one copy of the centre on yellow bond paper. Cut out and glue to middle of the cap top.
6. Make one copy of the topknot on yellow bond paper. Cut out the pattern. Score the tabs around the outside of the circle and score the four curved tabs and glue together. Then glue the rounded topknot to the middle of the cap as shown in the diagram.
7. Punch two small holes on opposite sides of the lower edge of the cap. Push the ends of the shoelace through the holes and tie knots on the inside.

Visual descriptions and patterns are on the next two pages.

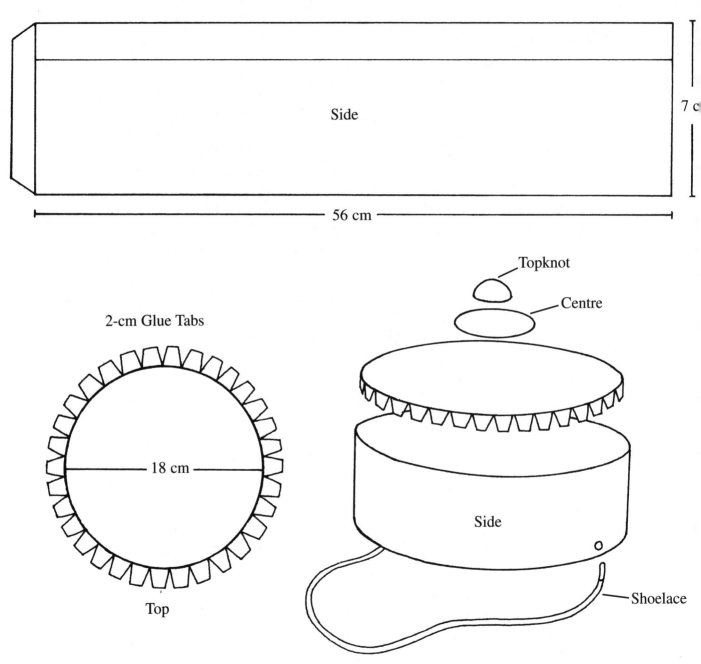

Side

7 cm

56 cm

2-cm Glue Tabs

18 cm

Top

Topknot

Centre

Side

Shoelace

18

Centre

Topknot

Photocopy these pieces on yellow paper.

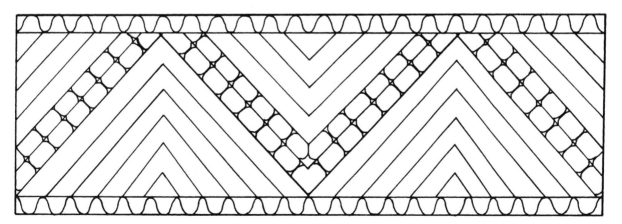

Copy 4 times.

CHAPTER 2 *Great Lone Land*

James Morrow Walsh, Acheson Gosford Irvine, and Others

After the long march west, the small force of only 300 Mounties had to patrol and enforce law and order in the massive Northwest Territories of Canada. They operated from the isolated forts and outposts that they established in the enormous, rugged wilderness. Individual police officers rode week-long patrols covering over 1100 km to protect the Canadian border and enforce justice.

James Morrow Walsh

"Bub" Walsh could run, swim, and fight better than any boy his size. In fact, he was good in all sports. He was the captain of the Prescott Lacrosse Team in 1869 when it won the world championship after defeating all Canadian and U.S. competitors.

When it came to school, James Walsh was not a great student. But he managed to graduate from the Royal Military College in Kingston, Ontario. When the Fenian raiders invaded Canada in 1866, James was one of the first to join the volunteers who pushed them back across the U.S. border. His commanding officer claimed he was "the best drilled Canadian to graduate and one of the best anywhere in action against those wild Irishmen known as Fenians."

James Walsh married Elizabeth Mowat and became the manager of the North American Hotel in Prescott, Ontario. In 1873, he left family and business behind to join the police force in the Northwest Territories.

Superintendent Walsh trained at Lower Fort Garry in Manitoba and travelled west with the Mounties. In 1875, Walsh led B Division into the heart of Blackfoot and Métis land in a broad valley close to the headwaters of Butte Creek. There he built a police fort, Fort Walsh.

Sitting Bull

In 1876, as Walsh was peacefully winning the trust of the Canadian Native people, an army general in the U.S. named George A. Custer was dealing harshly and violently with the Sioux nation led by Chief Sitting Bull. The confrontation ended in a battle at Little Big Horn, where Sitting Bull and his warriors massacred Custer and 225 blue-coated U.S. cavalry troops. Realizing that there would be greater numbers of American soldiers coming after him, Sitting Bull immediately gathered all his people and headed for Canada. They were bloody from the battle, brandishing weapons, and displaying trophies taken from their dead enemies. They arrived southeast of the Cypress Hills, in the territory patrolled by Superintendent Walsh.

Informed about the massacre south of the border, Walsh was patrolling the plains with some scouts when he encountered the first Sioux camp. The war chief of the camp was Four Horns. Noticing that Walsh was exhausted, Four Horns invited him to rest. To his amazement, Walsh accepted, stretched out on buffalo robes, and fell asleep. Never had a white person shown such bravery and trust as to sleep in a Sioux lodge. When he awoke, Walsh explained the Queen's laws that the Sioux would have to obey if they wished to remain in Canada.

Then a Sioux courier arrived. He accused Walsh of being a "Long-Knife American." Four Horns became distrustful. Calmly, Walsh announced that he and his scouts would stay overnight in the Sioux camp. He told Four Horns to send a few of his young warriors to a Native village 100 km away, where the people would vouch for Walsh as a friend. Four Horns agreed. The next day, Medicine Bear and Black Horn, with 200 warriors, rode into the Sioux camp, prepared for war if Walsh had been injured.

Soon afterwards, scouts reported that Sitting Bull had arrived in Canada. Superintendent Walsh, four other police officers, and a trusted Métis guide discovered Sitting Bull's camp of 5000 Sioux in the valley of Frenchman's Creek.

A Sioux warrior blocked their path at the edge of the camp. He warned them that they would die if they went any further. Walsh asked which teepee belonged to Sitting Bull, and led his small group into the camp. Sitting Bull gazed in amazement at the neatly dressed officer in his crimson tunic. Walsh offered a friendly handshake; Sitting Bull accepted it. Oblivious to the thousands of Sioux warriors, Walsh told Sitting Bull that he was in Canada and would have to obey Canadian laws.

Sitting Bull broke into laughter at the audacity of the white man. But he listened to Walsh's conditions for the Sioux remaining in Canada. The Mounties would protect them, but they could not use Canada as a refuge to continue waging war with the United States. They could not steal horses or cattle. If they did not obey Canadian laws, they would be jailed or forced to leave the country. As a sign of friendship and trust, Walsh and his men stayed overnight in the Sioux camp.

White Dog

The morning brought trouble. White Dog, an Assiniboine warrior from Missouri, rode into the camp with five stolen horses. Walsh confronted White Dog, threatening to arrest him. White Dog was hostile. Walsh remained calm but insistent. White Dog then claimed that he had found the horses wandering free. Walsh wisely seized on the sheepish excuse by allowing White Dog to go free with only a warning, but he confiscated the horses to emphasize his authority and power. Walsh later wrote: "White Dog was disgraced in the presence of the Sioux, and felt his position severely, but the lesson was long remembered by Bull and his followers."

Broken Arm

Three weeks after his meeting with Sitting Bull, Walsh received a complaint from Chief Little Cloud. His village teepees had been torn down, his horses shot, and women and children threatened by a band of Assiniboines from the U.S. led by Broken Arm. Walsh and a force of 25 Mounties discovered the Assiniboine camp and arrested Broken Arm and 25 of his warriors. But an alarm was sounded and the entire camp was aroused.

Pursued by hundreds of Assiniboines, Walsh took shelter on a hilltop, where he shackled his prisoners in pairs and built a fortress of stones. Four Assiniboine chiefs demanded that Walsh explain his actions. Walsh stated simply that they must obey the laws of Canada. The angry Native warriors eventually dispersed. In the trial back at his fort, James Walsh acted as both judge and jury. He sentenced Broken Arm to six months in jail.

End of an Era

At one time, tens of thousands of buffalo had grazed on the Canadian prairies. Their hides and carcasses had supplied shelter, clothing, and food for the Native people. Then careless hunters slaughtered the large herds, often just for sport. Native people were forced to live on government reserves. The Cree and Blackfoot chiefs signed treaties with the government to feed, clothe, and house their people on the reserves. The Sioux, who had fled north to escape the Americans, also needed help. But the government considered them refugees and encouraged them to return to the U.S.

American Offer

In October 1877, General A.H. Terry, leading three companies of American cavalry, escorted U.S. delegates to Fort Walsh to meet with Superintendent Macleod and Sitting Bull. Terry offered a "lasting peace" and full pardon to the Sioux if they gave up their guns and horses in exchange for life on reservations in the U.S. Sitting Bull and the other Sioux chiefs refused.

In July 1880, James Walsh was replaced by Superintendent Paddy Crozier. He visited the Sioux camps and patiently persuaded most of the Sioux chiefs to return to the U.S. Sitting Bull stubbornly resisted.

Acheson Gosford Irvine

In November 1880, James Macleod retired. Acheson Gosford Irvine became the third commissioner of the NWMP. Irvine, born in Canada and educated in Quebec, had been sent initially as an undercover agent to Montana when Macleod was dealing with the Hardwick Gang.

Irvine was a slim, chivalrous man. His first task was to persuade Sitting Bull to return south. After a winter of near starvation, Sitting Bull swallowed his pride and surrendered with his last 187 men, women, and children at Fort Buford in July 1881. Eleven years later, Sitting Bull was shot by Native police at Standing Rock, South Dakota.

Irvine recognized that the frontier era had ended. He updated the NWMP. He increased the size of the force to 500, issued better weapons and equipment, and created a permanent headquarters and training school in Regina. The NWMP became more professional under the command of Commissioner Irvine. The Mounties prepared for the era of the railway and new settlement on the western plains. Irvine would also have to deal with an eruption of rebel violence on the prairies.

Writing-On-Stone Police Post

During their long trek across the vast prairies in 1874, the Mounties discovered petroglyph and pictograph art carved in rock. The petroglyphs had been carved into the stone by prehistoric people using animal bones or pieces of antlers. The pictographs had been painted by mixing iron ore and water. The ironstone produced bright red, orange, and yellow images. They had been created over 3000 years earlier by the Blackfoot and other Native people in the Milk River Valley. The Mounties camped for four days at the magnificent site.

In 1887, the NWMP created a summer tent camp at Writing-On-Stone, and in 1889, wooden buildings were constructed as part of the boundary patrol that stretched from Manitoba to the Rocky Mountains.

Slippery Ann and Mountie Magic

When the news of Sitting Bull's victory over General Custer reached Canada, Bub Walsh was on sick leave. He returned immediately with 35 new recruits. Their river steamer became grounded on a sandbar, so they set out on foot.

They met a long-haired, rugged frontiersman in a fringed buckskin jacket who was known as Slippery Ann. Walsh immediately hired him as a guide.

On the way to Fort Walsh, they encountered a band of Crow families who were peaceful until some of the inexperienced recruits began to flirt with the Native women. The situation became dangerous; the outnumbered Mounties were certain to lose in any confrontation.

Slippery Ann came to their rescue. Earlier he had observed a young Mountie named Andy Grogan doing magic tricks. He told the Crow that the Mountie "medicine man" would perform. With Slippery Ann as interpreter, Andy asked a warrior on horseback what his horse ate. The Crow replied bluntly, "Grass." Andy announced, "This pony has eaten something else." Then he pulled a dozen pocket knives from the horse's mouth. The Native audience shouted and whooped, declaring that Andy was the devil. Slippery Ann assured the Mounties that Andy's magic had saved their lives.

Doctor and Artist

Richard Barrington Nevitt was an American who had escaped from the violence of the American Civil War to study medicine in Toronto. He became the assistant surgeon with the Mounties on their trek west in 1874.

Nevitt gained the trust of the Blackfoot as their doctor and immortalized them by painting their portraits and capturing their way of life.

Create a Mountie Booklet, DVD, or Web Page

The real-life stories of brave and courageous Mounties are more exciting and entertaining than stories of fictional heroes found in books, on television, at movies, or obtained off the Internet. Using personalities, events, and images from this book, library resources, or the Internet, create a personal description of your Mountie hero.

What you need:
- information and images from a library or on the Internet
- pen, pencil, photocopier, video camera, or computer

What to do:
1. Research a Mountie hero of your choice.
2. Write your own description of the Mountie, emphasizing why you consider the person a hero.
3. Obtain photographs or images of the person and images representing the events in which he or she was involved.
4. Using your description and images, create a booklet, a DVD, or a Web page about your Mountie hero.
5. Footnote the sources of your information and images. Provided that you are using your own description and not creating a commercial product, there should be no copyright problems.
6. Share your creation with your family, friends, or classmates.

3 *Railway and Settlement*

Sam Steele, William Wilde, Billy Fury, and Others

By 1878, thousands of new settlers had arrived in the Northwest Territories. They congregated outside police forts, such as Fort Walsh, Fort Macleod, and Fort Saskatchewan. Hundreds of people lived in the village beside Fort Walsh, providing the Mounties with essential services and goods. Native people camped nearby, attracted by the opportunity to trade with the townspeople.

Battleford had been named the territorial capital in 1876 and was growing rapidly. A telegraph line connected Battleford to Fort Pelly and Winnipeg. In 1877, the telegraph line reached Edmonton, which had a population of almost 1000 people. The *Saskatchewan Herald* became the first newspaper in the territory in 1878.

Railway Construction

From 1881 to 1883, the new railway construction created jobs and brought a steady flow of settlers. The first train from the east had arrived at Winnipeg in 1877. After William Van Horne was made the general manager of the Canadian Pacific Railway (CPR) in 1881, he accelerated the construction across the western plains.

By October, the track had reached Brandon. The next year, it was extended to Regina, which had become the new capital of the territory. By 1883, it had reached the frontier post of Calgary. New towns, such as Medicine Hat,

Moose Jaw, and Swift Current, were created along the railway's route. In 1881, the population of the Northwest Territories was 7000 white settlers, 5000 Métis, and between 20,000 and 30,000 Native people. By 1884, the white population had increased to more than 23,000.

Policing the Rails

The Native leaders feared and distrusted the railway, the iron demon they called the "fire wagon."

More than 5000 railway workers arrived on the western plains in the early 1880s. When the railway crews reached the Cypress Hills in the winter of 1882-1883, a Cree chief named Piapot sent warriors to uproot 64 km of railway survey stakes, and pitched his camp on the railway right-of-way. Two crimson-coated Mounties arrived on black horses. Corporal William Brock Wilde gave Piapot 15 minutes to move the human blockade. The Native warriors threatened the two Mounties. When the time was up, Wilde dismounted, marched up to Piapot's teepee, and pulled it down on the heads of the women inside. He then proceeded through the Cree camp and knocked down all of the buffalo-skin lodges. Because he admired the courage of the young Mountie, Chief Piapot ordered his followers to pick up their belongings and leave the railway lands.

Chief Crowfoot reacted angrily when construction workers arrived on his Blackfoot reserve east of Calgary. The Canadian government had told him that the lands would belong to his people forever. The government had signed a treaty, but then it came to build a railway across his reserve. With over 700 warriors ready to attack, he confronted the railway crew. Father Albert Lacombe, a Roman Catholic missionary, used his friendship with Crowfoot to avoid bloodshed. In place of war, the wise Crowfoot negotiated. He agreed to the railway construction in exchange for additional lands.

Railway Boom Towns

By late 1883, the CPR had reached the Rocky Mountains. Life in the railway construction camps was rough and dangerous. Drinking and gambling frequently led to violent conflicts. Inspector Samuel B. Steele was placed in charge of a detachment of Mounties. They were ordered to follow the railway crews and enforce the Act for the Preservation of Peace in the Vicinity of Public Works, which outlawed drinking and gambling within a 16-km radius of the railway line. Beyond the 16-km "no trespassing zone," wild boom towns developed. Merchants, saloon keepers, dance hall women, and gamblers prospered from the wages of the railway workers.

In 1883, the first serious strike broke out when the CPR reduced the wages of its engineers and firemen. Mounties were quickly sent to Moose Jaw and

Broadview to protect railway property, as well as the non-striking workers, from the brawling protesters.

In 1885, another violent strike occurred at Beaver Crossing. Over 1200 men quit working over a wage dispute. A mob of 300 furious protesters tried to stop a trainload of non-striking workers. But the boss, James Ross, drove the locomotive through the strikers with bullets whizzing past his ears. Sam Steele was seriously ill and unable to get out of his bed. He could spare only four Mounties, led by Sergeant Billy Fury, to protect the workers. Fury faced hundreds of angry, shouting rioters who were firing guns into the air. The sergeant was not intimidated. He threatened to shoot anyone who tried to pass his small detachment of men. The mob retreated.

Another problem erupted. A Mountie trying to arrest a suspect in the lawless shantytown was attacked. Steele sent Fury and his men to make the arrest. Fury disappeared into the boom town, and then a shot was heard. Steele crawled to the window of his cabin to see the four constables with their prisoner being pursued by a threatening gang of workers. Ignoring his illness, Sam Steele grabbed a rifle and rushed out to defend his men. He warned the troublemakers to keep their hands off their guns. Steele's assistant read the Riot Act, which gave the Mounties the official authority to use any force necessary. As eight constables cocked their rifles behind him, Steele warned the strikers that he would open fire on any group of 12 or more who assembled in public. The demonstrators dispersed.

The railway eventually paid the overdue wages, but the ringleaders of the mutiny were fined $100 or given six months of hard labour.

Early Ranchers
In 1874, a gold miner brought a herd of 25 Texas cattle from Montana to the settlement of Morley. John Shaw brought a herd of 450 cattle through the

mountains from British Columbia in 1875. He supplied beef to the Mounties at Fort Calgary and gradually sold off his entire herd by 1876.

Some former whisky traders, such as Fred Kanouse and William Henry Lee, switched from selling alcohol to the Native people to supplying Mounties and fur traders with milk and beef. In 1886, Joseph McFarland built the Pioneer Ranch east of Fort Macleod after herding dairy cattle from Montana so he could trade with the Mounties.

By 1879, most of the great buffalo herds had been eradicated from the Canadian prairies. The fertile soil of the Saskatchewan plains and the rich green foothills of Alberta attracted cowboys with their cattle.

Mountie Cowboys

Mounties who came west in 1874 had signed contracts to serve in the force for five years. In 1878, many left the force and became the first Canadian cowboys. Former Mountie Edward Maunsell, originally from Ireland, brought 100 cows and three bulls from Montana in 1879. More than 1000 head of cattle existed near Fort Macleod. Other Mounties who became cowboys included Jim Bell, Bob Patterson, and John D. Miller. Some entrepreneurial Mounties, such as Sam Steele, Percy Neale, William Winder, and Albert Shurtliff, became ranchers as a sideline while still serving on the force.

Disappearing Cattle

In 1879, half of the cattle mysteriously disappeared. Angry ranchers were convinced that hungry Native people, whose buffalo herds had been exterminated, were responsible. They asked Commissioner Macleod for permission to shoot cattle thieves. He told them that if they did, they would be hanged, and he refused to compensate them for their lost animals. The cowboys took their herds to Montana until they could be better protected.

Return of the Cowboys

By 1881, the Canadian government had signed land treaties and was supplying the Native reserves with food. It issued grazing leases to ranchers. A rancher could lease up to 40,000 hectares of grazing land at one cent for every two and a half hectares per year for 21 years. The Mounties, acting as police, judges, and jailers, would protect the ranchers. Large and small ranches flourished as the cowboys returned with their herds. In 1880, there were about 1000 cattle in the territory, but by 1881, there were 6000, and by 1882, the herds had expanded to 16,000.

Canadian cowboys were not any different than the American cowboys; in fact, the majority of them were Americans who had migrated north. Because the Mounties had established law and order, the cowboys who drifted north to Canada didn't need to resort to hanging horse thieves, gun duels in the streets, or range wars over territory – all common events in the American west.

The new railway lines enabled cowboys to ship their cattle to eastern Canada and Europe. But the railway also brought competitors for the land. As settlers and farmers arrived from the east, the cowboy era ended.

Free Farmland

In 1896, Clifford Sifton, Canada's minister of the interior, initiated an international advertising campaign to entice settlers to the western plains. Brochures that praised the quality of the land for growing agricultural crops were circulated in the U.S. and Europe. The Canadian government offered free land grants of 65 hectares plus special prices on sea and rail transportation to farmers who would come to the Canadian territory.

By 1914, over a million settlers had responded and were living on the prairies. About one-third were from European countries, such as Germany, Finland, Sweden, Russia, and the Ukraine.

The Mounties were available to help and give advice. Often the new Canadians could not speak English, so interpreters were needed. The Mounties became land agents and agricultural experts. They offered advice on crop requirements, soil qualities, and livestock fitness. They met new immigrants at the train stations, took them out to choose a land site, and supplied assistance and, if necessary, welfare.

The wives of the Mounties were also very active in introducing the immigrants and their families to the country. They helped the new arrivals adapt to life on the Canadian prairies.

Naked Protestors
Sometimes the new settlers caused unusual problems that the Mounties were

expected to solve. In 1899, thousands of Doukhobor farmers arrived from Russia, where their religious beliefs had caused confrontations with authorities. They were good farmers, but they refused to speak English or obey Canadian laws that they didn't like. They caused problems with other new settlers. The Mounties were sent to deal with the conflicts.

The Doukhobors demanded religious rights and their own schools. Religious beliefs prompted one group of Doukhobors, the Sons of Freedom, to protest by throwing off all their clothes. They began naked protest marches, which included singing hymns. When confronted, they went on hunger strikes and refused to eat, or to feed their children. The Mounties removed the children, forced the adults to dress, placed some in insane asylums, and force-fed the starving. The Doukhobors responded by rioting. They threw stones at the police and attacked them with clubs.

In the cold winter of 1902, over a thousand Sons of Freedom marched in protest from Yorkton to Minnedosa, Manitoba, without food or clothing. Inspector J.O. Wilson and a detachment of 20 Mounties were assigned to watch over them. When the government gave the order that they were to be returned home, the Mounties had to board the sometimes violent protesters onto trains for the return trip to Yorkton.

Doukhobor protests continued for more than 50 years. Between March 1952 and March 1953, the Mounties investigated over 60 fires and dynamite explosions that destroyed hydro lines and railway tracks near Doukhobor settlements. In 1971, they were still refusing to obey laws, causing disturbances, and participating in hunger strikes when imprisoned.

Train Robbers

Train robberies were common in the U.S., but rare in Canada. In May 1906, three American outlaws, Bill Minor, William Dunn, and Shorty Colquhoun, robbed a CPR train near Kamloops, British Columbia. Sergeant J.J. Wilson with four other Mounties picked up the trail of the bandits, who were heading back towards the U.S. border.

Pursuing them on horseback through a cold, pelting rainstorm, the Mounties discovered the three desperadoes huddled around a camp fire. When Wilson tried to place them under arrest, William Dunn started shooting and ran into the forest. Minor and Colquhoun also tried to pull their weapons, but the armed Mounties stopped them. Two police officers chased after Dunn. Shots were exchanged, and Dunn was hit in the leg. After the wounded outlaw was bandaged, the three robbers were taken to Kamloops and given long prison sentences.

Canadian Cowgirl

Annie Armstrong had a herd of beef and dairy cattle. Her hired foreman was O.H. Morgan. Like other Canadian ranchers protesting the lack of Mountie protection against cattle thieves, she took her herd to Montana.

In Montana, a cowboy named Brackett E. Stewart shot Annie and Morgan, then looted and burned their ranch. Annie's daughters, 12-year-old Maggie and six-year-old Annie, were outside when they heard the shots and hid until the killer left. Then they ran to the deputy sheriff, who also owned a local store. As Maggie was telling her story, she suddenly screamed and pointed to a cowboy who had just entered the crowded store. "There's the man who killed my mother!"

Stewart was arrested and locked in a storeroom until the deputy could send for a judge. Before the judge arrived, a posse of over 20 masked vigilantes took the prisoner at gunpoint from the deputy and hanged him from a tree. It was American frontier justice, not Mountie-style justice.

4 *Prairie Rebels*

Paddy Crozier, Francis Dickens, and Others

The railway opened up the western prairies by bringing thousands of new settlers to the frontier towns. The Métis who lived along the South Saskatchewan River became worried about the loss of their lands and lifestyle. Canadian government surveyors were ignoring their traditional land rights on the riverfront. The Métis appealed to the government in Ottawa, but were ignored.

The North-West Rebellion

Gabriel Dumont, the Métis leader, took action. He invited Louis Riel, who had led a Métis rebellion in Manitoba in 1869, to come back from exile in Montana to aid in the fight to save their lands in Saskatchewan. In 1885, Riel defied authorities by setting up his own government, with Dumont as the commander of the Métis force. The Cree, led by Chief Poundmaker and Chief Big Bear, joined the Métis revolt against the intruders. Macleod's friend, Chief Crowfoot, and his Blackfoot warriors refused to participate.

Trek to Fort Carlton

In March 1885, reports of the hostilities about to erupt in the north came from Superintendent Paddy Crozier* at Fort Carlton. The news prompted Commissioner Irvine to march north from Regina with a force of four officers, 86 men, and 66 horses. In the middle of winter, the column of Mountie sleighs

---

* Paddy Crozier had been the first Mountie to make an arrest when he captured William Bond's gang of whisky traders.

pressed its way through snowstorms in freezing weather. During the gruelling 20-km trek that took seven days, some men suffered from frostbite, and others went snowblind. Before they reached Fort Carlton, the bloody rebellion had begun.

Duck Lake Disaster

On March 26, 1885, leading a force of 56 Mounties and 43 Prince Albert Volunteers, Paddy Crozier left Fort Carlton to retrieve food and ammunition left by a trader escaping from the rebels at Duck Lake. Gabriel Dumont, who was known as the Prince of the Plains, was waiting for them with an army of 350 Métis. Surrounded and outnumbered, the Mounties and the volunteers struggled in the deep snowdrifts as their enemies were sniping at them from behind trees. Many of their horses were shot, 12 men were killed, and another 12 wounded. The Mounties were forced to retreat.

During the slaughter, an unarmed Louis Riel rode through the chaos, dressed in a black robe and waving a crucifix in his hand, to urge on his men. Dumont was wounded, but recovered quickly. His instinct was to destroy the vulnerable Mountie force struggling back to Fort Carlton, but Louis Riel objected to more bloodshed.

Retreat to Prince Albert

The same day that Crozier's defeated men reached Fort Carlton, A.G. Irvine and his force of 90 Mounties, exhausted from their long journey, arrived. Irvine made the decision to abandon the isolated fort and set up a headquarters at the heavily populated community of Prince Albert. An accidental fire broke out; Fort Carlton was in flames as they hastily evacuated it at 4 a.m.

The parade of Mounties stretched more than 3 km as it moved slowly through the snow towards Prince Albert. Again Dumont urged Riel to attack

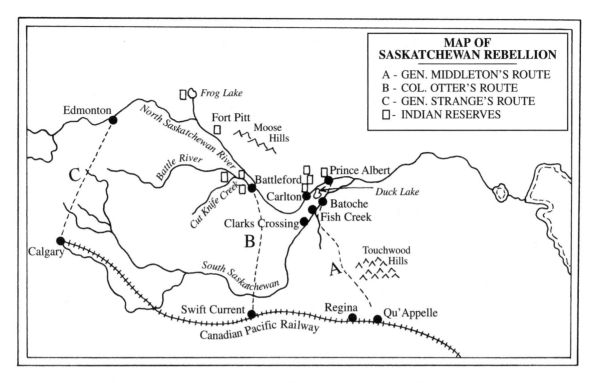

and annihilate the exposed column of Mounties; again Riel refused.

At Prince Albert, Commissioner Irvine established his headquarters in a church, around which he built a wooden stockade that was 3 m high. Irvine received a telegraph message from Ottawa that Major-General Frederick D. Middleton was on his way with an army of 2000, and that the general would take command when he arrived. Middleton's huge army was transported from eastern Canada on the new CPR railway in a few days.

Frog Lake Massacre

Inspector Francis Dickens was in command of 25 Mounties at Fort Pitt. He was the third son of the famous English author Charles Dickens. He had previously served with the Bengal Police in India. Francis Dickens had come west with

Commissioner French in 1874. He was thin and sported a stylish red beard.

Fort Pitt was located about 56 km from Frog Lake, where a smaller detachment of Mounties under Corporal R.B. Sleigh was stationed. Tom Quinn was the government agent in charge of the Cree community at Frog Lake. Hearing that the Cree under Chief Big Bear might join forces with the Métis rebels, Dickens suggested to Quinn that the white settlers at Frog Lake should come to Fort Pitt for protection, or that more Mounties should be sent to Frog Lake. Quinn, a Métis of Sioux blood, refused both suggestions. Because he believed the police presence was antagonizing Big Bear, Quinn sent the Mounties at Frog Lake back to Fort Pitt.

Chief Big Bear had refused Quinn's efforts to have his Cree people settle on a reserve and accept government assistance. Big Bear knew that war would destroy his people; he believed in passive resistance. Yet the old chief could not control his eager young warriors. On April 2, 1885, his war chief, Wandering Spirit, attacked Frog Lake. The Native warriors killed Tom Quinn and seven other settlers as they looted the community.

Big Bear was furious. He scolded the hotheaded warriors and prevented Wandering Spirit from killing other white settlers who had been taken as prisoners. Eleven days after the Frog Lake massacre, Big Bear and 250 Crees camped close to Fort Pitt. Big Bear told Inspector Dickens that his young men were out of his control. He begged the Mountie to abandon the fort, explaining that his warriors were determined to burn it down.

The situation escalated when two Mounties on patrol were pursued by a war party. Constable D.L. Cowan fell from his galloping horse and was killed as he ran towards the fort; Constable C. Loasby, wounded in the leg, had his horse shot out from under him. Lone Man, Big Bear's son-in-law, shot him in the back, but Loasby limped to the safety of the fort.

Big Bear offered Dickens and his men a peaceful retreat if they left Fort Pitt. The Mounties deserted the fort in a heavy, early-morning snowstorm, travelled 160 km down the icy Saskatchewan River in a leaking scow for seven days, and reached Fort Battleford. There Dickens learned that Chief Poundmaker's Cree warriors had joined the Métis rebellion by looting and burning the settlement of Battleford on March 30, 1885.

Rebel Resistance

General Middleton, leading his army north from the CPR line, clashed with Dumont's Métis force at Fish Creek. Although the army had cannons and gatling guns, the Métis rebels were not defeated, and Middleton had to wait for reinforcements.

Another army detachment, commanded by Lieutenant-Colonel W.D. Otter, arrived at Battleford and continued 50 km west to confront Chief Poundmaker at Cut Knife Hill. One-third of the force was 75 Mounties led by Superintendents W.M. Herchmer and Percy R. Neale. The attack failed; eight soldiers and six warriors died. Otter retreated back to Fort Battleford.

Gatling Gun

Defeat at Batoche

General Middleton renewed his attack and confronted Dumont's rebels at Batoche in May 1885. After three days of bloody fighting, the Métis ran out of ammunition. The determined defenders dug in and substituted nails, stones, and metal buttons for bullets. They were defeated on May 12. Dumont escaped south to the U.S., but Louis Riel was captured.

After trials at Battleford, Wandering Spirit and seven other Native warriors were hanged. Poundmaker and Big Bear were sentenced to three years at Manitoba's Stoney Mountain Penitentiary. Both were released early, but they both died soon after being freed. Louis Riel was tried for high treason and was hanged in Regina on November 16, 1885.

Almighty Voice

By the end of the century, from 1890 to 1900, settlement on the prairies had replaced the frontier days. Most First Nations had signed treaties and lived on government reserves. But mavericks and renegades still endangered the communities and the lives of citizens and police officers.

In 1896, a young Cree named Almighty Voice was living in poverty on a northern reserve 6.5 km northeast of Batoche. Unlike his father and other band members, he chose to live as a hunter, rather than a farmer. When Almighty Voice was arrested for killing a cow and sent to the NWMP detachment at Duck Lake, he escaped.

Sergeant C.C. Colebrook and a Métis scout tracked him down. The Mountie tried to persuade the desperate fugitive to surrender, but was shot off his horse and killed. Almighty Voice instantly became the focus of a massive manhunt. He was joined by his brother-in-law, Tupean, and his 13-year-old cousin, Going-Up-to-Sky. For over a year, they eluded the police.

In one encounter, a police scout was wounded in the shoulder; in another, Sergeant Raven was shot in his leg and Inspector Jack Allen was hit in his right arm. Trapped on a bluff, the three young Native men dug a pit in the ground. When Corporal Charles Hockin led seven men in an attack, he and two others were killed. About 100 police and volunteers surrounded the bluff and bombarded it with cannon fire. When the barrage ended, the body of Tupean was discovered, shot in the head. Going-Up-to-Sky and Almighty Voice had been killed by cannon fire in their pit.

Charcoal

In 1896, a Blood warrior in the south named Charcoal went on a killing spree. He discovered one of his wives, Pretty Wolverine Woman, with her lover, Medicine Pipe Stem, and shot the man dead. He immediately went to the house of Chief Red Crow, intending to kill him, but dogs warned of his approach. Next he sought to kill Indian Agent James Wilson, but no one was at home. His third target was a white man, Edward McNeil, the farm instructor for the reserve. Charcoal shot McNeil through a window, wounding him in the back.

Charcoal forced six family members to escape south with him. His prisoners were his two wives, a mother-in-law, a teenaged daughter, and two stepchildren. When Inspector A.M. "Buzz" Jarvis caught up with him, the Mountie was grazed on his skull by a bullet. Charcoal stole some police horses to escape.

An angry Inspector Sam Steele took command of the operation. He arrested 25 members of Charcoal's family, including his two brothers, Bear Back Bone and Left Hand. Steele released them only after they promised to help capture their criminal brother.

Sergeant William Wilde, who had forced Chief Piapot off the CPR lands in 1883, tracked down Charcoal and charged at him. But Wilde was shot from his horse and wounded in the side. Charcoal murdered the fallen police officer with a point-blank shot and stole his horse. When the dangerous maverick returned to the Blood Reserve, his two brothers captured him and delivered the killer to Sam Steele. Charcoal was hanged for murder on March 16, 1897.

Lost Watch

Inspector Francis Dickens had left his gold watch behind when he hastily evacuated Fort Pitt. The watch was recovered by Dickens many years later when a Métis offered it for sale.

Wild West Show

After he escaped to the U.S., Gabriel Dumont became an entertainer in Buffalo Bill Cody's Wild West Show, re-enacting his battles with the NWMP. Another member of the acting company was Chief Sitting Bull, who dramatized the massacre of General Custer's cavalry at Little Big Horn.

Rebel or Madman?

Louis Riel, who had spent two years in insane asylums, convinced himself that God was commanding him and regarded himself as the Prophet of the New World. He believed that he had been summoned by his Métis people to save them. Because of his strange attire and behaviour, many believed he was insane. Yet he refused his lawyer's suggestion that he plead insanity at his trial for high treason.

Kootenay Rebels

In 1887, trouble erupted in British Columbia. Members of the Kootenay First Nation raided the provincial jail at Wild Horse and released a Native prisoner who had been charged with the murders of white miners.

Superintendent Sam Steele arrived from Fort Walsh with three officers and 75 men to quell the insurrection. It took several months to establish order again. The Mounties finally were able to leave in August 1888.

Tracking and Observation

The Mounties' ability to recognize tracks and make proper deductions from them was one of their most important skills. They often followed criminals or lost individuals over vast tracts of wilderness.

What you need:
- heavy tape
- a coin
- small bits of paper
- notepad and pencil

What to do:
Have a friend make a trail following one of these methods.
1. On soft ground: Tape a coin to the bottom of one of your friend's shoes. He or she walks for 20 minutes, or about 1 km, and then stops. As the tracker, you follow the trail until you find your friend.
2. On hard ground: Your friend drops small pieces of paper on the ground every 20 or 30 paces, leaving a trail to follow. As the tracker, you pick up the paper along the trail until you find your friend.

Tracking Animals

Tracking animals can also be fun. Dogs or cats can easily be tracked after a light snowfall. Tracking wild animals is more difficult. Your dog will be able to smell a trail that your eye cannot detect and can follow that trail for great distances.

Use notepaper to write down what you observe as you track animals. Observe tracks of other creatures, type of ground, and weather conditions.

In the City

If you live in a city where tracking is difficult, you can still develop skills of careful observation.

What to do:

With a friend, choose four different store-window displays in a mall. Stand in front of each window for one minute, carefully observing the objects in the window. Go around the corner and write down all the things you can remember from the display. Return to the window and check your lists. Do the same for the other three windows. Tally your scores at the end to find out who has the best observation skills.

5 *Yukon Gold and Arctic Patrols*

Klondike Kate, Zac Wood, Denny LaNauze, and Others

In the Canadian north, a new challenge emerged for the NWMP in the cold, barren Yukon. Gold was discovered close to the Alaska border on the Forty Mile Creek, which was a small tributary of the Yukon River.

Greedy for gold, Americans swarmed north to Skagway and Dyea in Alaska, then across the border into the Yukon. Canadians and adventurers from Europe and other parts of the world also came to the Yukon territory via Alaska. The rush of gold-hungry strangers set off a chain reaction. The previously peaceful territory was inundated with fortune seekers, called "stampeders," and traders and merchants keen to serve them.

Miners needed to know that their discoveries would not be stolen. Anglican ministers were concerned about protecting the Native people from the influx of liquor merchants. The government had to ensure that the Yukon remained Canadian territory. The task of maintaining law and order became the responsibility of the Mounties.

In 1886, Lawrence William Herchmer had become the fourth commissioner of the NWMP. He sent Inspector Charles Constantine and Staff Sergeant Charles Best to the Yukon in 1894. Their job was to assure the residents, new and old, that the Canadian government was there to protect them. Travelling by boat and on horseback, the two Mounties took two and a half months to reach Fort Cudahy, close to the town of Forty Mile.

Native people made up the largest part of the population of the Yukon when the Mounties arrived. Of the 1000 merchants, fur trappers, and miners, only 260 were actually miners. They produced about $300,000 in gold in 1893; by 1898, more than $6,000,000 was being produced yearly. The citizens came from many countries, but about 80 percent were Americans.

Charles Constantine anticipated problems over the registration of the mining claims. He recommended that 50 men be sent to the Yukon. He emphasized that the Mounties chosen for the assignment should be large and powerful, be experienced, and abstain from drinking alcohol. But when the Canadian government created the Yukon District as part of the Northwest Territories in July 1895, Constantine was given only 19 men. He built Fort Constantine, the first NWMP fort in the Yukon.

Gold Rush Panic

The new fort was barely built when chaos erupted. Three miners, George Washington Carmack and his two Native partners, Skookum Jim and Tagish Charley, discovered gold on Rabbit Creek. They registered the claim with Charles Constantine on August 21, 1896. It was valued at 30 times the quality of other Yukon gold. Rabbit Creek, 80 km east of Forty Mile, was renamed Bonanza Creek. Miners deserted Forty Mile to rush upriver. Over 100,000 eagerly set out for the goldfields; most turned back disenchanted.

The 19 Mounties could not handle the invasion of tens of thousands of gold-crazed miners swarming into the Yukon, all of them expecting instant wealth. From 1896 to November 1898, the number of Mounties in the Yukon increased from 19 to 285.

In February 1898, Commissioner Herchmer sent Superintendent A.B. Perry to create Mountie posts on the Alaska-Yukon border. The 31 detachments of Mounties were reorganized into H and B divisions.

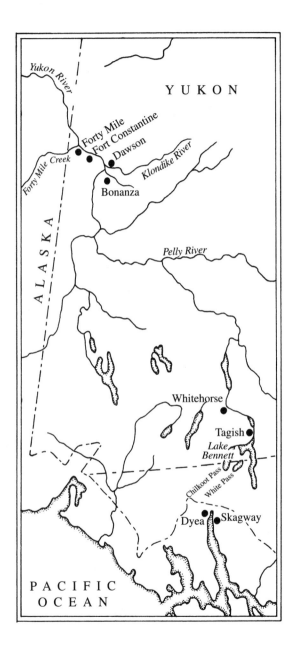

Dead Horse Trail and the Golden Stairs

Superintendent Sam Steele came from Fort Macleod to command the gateway to the goldfields. Fortune seekers entered Canada through two passes, which were 1800 m up in the mountains. Tent camps and wooden shacks housed the Mounties guarding the towering entrance to the Yukon territory.

Inspector D'Arcy Strickland led the White Pass detachment on the dangerous Dead Horse Trail from Skagway, Alaska. It got its nickname from the 3000 pack animals that died along the route.

Inspector "Bobbie" Belcher led the Chilkoot Pass detachment at the peak of the 1500 Golden Stairs. Carved from snow and ice, the Golden Stairs were part of the exhausting 300-m climb from Dyea, Alaska. The Mounties' jobs were collecting customs duties and ensuring that the gold miners had sufficient supplies to survive for a year. They inspected the outfits of the new arrivals. One person

could carry about 25 kg, but he or she required 1000 kg of supplies to survive. Pack animals had to be used. Robbery and murder were common in the Alaska towns, but miners put their weapons away when they crossed into Canadian territory.

Blizzards, snow that was 18 m deep, and freezing temperatures hampered the Mounties. People became ill from typhoid fever. Food was so scarce that starvation became a threat. When Sam Steele heard that D'Arcy Strickland had bronchitis, he climbed up the White Pass and ordered him off duty. Sam had bronchitis himself, yet stubbornly continued to work.

On the Canadian side of the passes at Lake Bennett, Sam established his base of operations. There he found over 10,000 stampeders camped in tents and building boats to sail to the Klondike after the spring thaw.

The Great Boat Race

On May 29, 1898, the boat race to Dawson City on the Klondike River began. Thousands of vessels of every description, carrying passengers eager to reach the goldfields and stake their claims, rushed across Lake Bennett. Sam Steele ensured that each craft had a number painted on it to keep track of everyone during the dangerous journey.

When they reached the Whitehorse Rapids at the head of the canyon, 150 boats were destroyed in the swirling waters and 10 men drowned. A corporal named Dixon and his men, experienced in swift-water travel, saved many lives. Steele instantly made a new law. No boat could continue without a qualified guide who was approved by Corporal Dixon. Women and children would travel around the rapids on foot with police protection.

Paris of the North

In 1887, Dawson City was just a Native fishing camp. After shimmering gold nuggets in the sandy creek beds attracted the attention of miners, it became the largest city west of Winnipeg and north of Victoria. Fort Herchmer, built at Dawson City in 1897, became the new NWMP headquarters, from which Sam Steele commanded B Division.

By 1898, the population of Dawson had expanded to over 30,000. Gold nuggets and bags of gold dust were the accepted currency. Dawson was called the Paris of the North. Ornate hotels, flashy dance halls, lavish theatres, motion picture shows, and elaborate riverboats replaced the wilderness. Electricity, telephone service, running water, and steam heat civilized the isolated city. Citizens strolled along boardwalks above the muddy streets. Banks, stores, churches, and an expensive library were built.

Sam Steele ensured that the dance halls and barrooms, filled with thieves, con artists, and gamblers, were kept under control. Compared to lawless communities in Alaska, such as Skagway, Dawson City was safe and peaceful. Women and children walked without fear through the streets, even at night. Sam Steele never needed to fire his weapon.

Women of the Gold Rush

Although vastly outnumbered by men, thousands of women lived in Dawson City. Many adventurers brought wives and children with them. Independent women braved the northern elements and survived the primitive life. Women entertainers and others were also attracted by the gold in Dawson City.

Newspapers told stories about Ethel Bush Berry, "the bride of the Klondike," who crossed over the Chilkoot Pass in a dogsled team with her husband Clarence. Their claim on Eldorado Creek earned $1.5 million dollars.

Martha Purdy, an American on her way to the Yukon, decided to separate from her husband. Even though she was pregnant, she continued alone, staked a lucrative claim, purchased a sawmill business, married a lawyer named George Black, and became known as the First Lady of the Yukon. Martha Purdy Black was the second woman to be elected as a member of the Canadian Parliament and the first to represent the Yukon.

Another single mother, Beatrice Lorne from Australia, was dubbed the Klondike Nightingale. In a superb soprano voice, she sang nostalgic songs.

Nuns and nurses also came to the Yukon. Three nuns, the Sisters of St. Ann, arrived in 1898 to aid Father William Judge, who had built Dawson's Catholic church in 1897. The nuns raised money for St. Mary's Hospital by seeking donations of gold nuggets.

Four Canadian women of the Victorian Order of Nurses helped with the deadly outbreaks of typhoid fever. These epidemics were caused by the lack of a sewer system and garbage collection in Dawson City.

A rare occupation for a woman in 1898 was newspaper reporting. Flora Shaw was an experienced journalist for *The Times* of London, England. Operating from a primitive tent, Flora trudged through the mining camps, reporting to the world that 5000 miners were discovering $6,000,000 in gold and complaining about the government's 10 percent royalty on their findings.

Young Frances Dorley from Seattle convinced her parents to let her risk the trip to the goldfields. To reach the Yukon, she worked as a cook for stampeders. In Dawson, she opened a roadhouse restaurant in the heart of the goldfields and made a fortune serving homemade meals.

Belinda Mulrooney was called "the richest woman in the Klondike." When the entrepreneurial Belinda arrived in Dawson, she threw her last 25-cent coin into the Yukon River for good luck. With her ceaseless energy and enterprising personality, she made her fortune opening lavish hotels and restaurants, such as the Grand Forks and the Fairview hotels.

Kate Carmack's fate was not so prosperous. Her husband, "Lying" George, and her brother, Skookum Jim, found gold and became millionaires. At first, Kate, whose Native name was *Shaaw Tlaa*, shared the rich life, gave birth to a daughter, and journeyed to Seattle. But her marriage was never official. George remarried and left Kate penniless.

Woman Constable

More than a dozen women in the Yukon were given the nickname "Klondike Kate." Two of them became legends.

The most impressive Klondike Kate was born in Johnville, New Brunswick, as Katherine Ryan on August 20, 1869. She became a nurse in Seattle but was lured to the Klondike, where she staked three gold claims. The NWMP hired Kate as a special constable. She was one of the first females on the force.* Kate became a gold inspector, collecting royalties on the nuggets. She also worked as a jailer, ran a restaurant, and became involved in local politics as an early suffragette. She often used her nursing skills to heal men injured in vicious barroom fights.

A second Klondike Kate was an entertainer from the United States. Kathleen Rockwell was born in Junction City, Kansas, in 1876. She was also known as "the Flame of the Yukon." During her famous flame dance, she wore a dress with sparkling red sequins. She ran, jumped, and swirled across the stage with 180 m of red chiffon flowing around her like flames. The miners threw gold nuggets or bags of gold dust on the stage in appreciation. Kate was also famous for her love affairs and marriages.

Yukon Legends

Sam Steele and other Mounties became legends of the Yukon. They met many other legendary personalities in Dawson City. The poet Robert Service lived in a cabin on a hill above the city. He called the Yukon "the land of the midnight sun" and created mythical characters such as Sam McGee, who was based on a real citizen of Dawson. Another writer was Jack London, the author of *Call of the Wild*, a famous novel about a dog named Buck. The hero in the story

* The NWMP employed women as early as the 1880s. In 1897, an Order-in-Council allowed for the employment of women jailers to escort women prisoners in the Northwest Territories. Native and Inuit women, as well as the wives of Mounties, were hired.

was named after a dog that was owned by Belinda Mulrooney, the woman who opened the Fairview Hotel in Dawson.

Millionaire miner Charley Anderson was known as "the Lucky Swede." The richest miner was Big Alex McDonald. Fred Trump, grandfather of billionaire Donald Trump, operated the Arctic Restaurant and Hotel.

"Swiftwater Bill" Gates was not related to the Internet billionaire Bill Gates, but he had the same talent for making million-dollar deals and investments. He also lost fortunes as quickly as he created them because of his addiction to gambling and fascination with young dance hall women.

Canadian legend Joe Boyle arrived in the goldfields without any money. He laboured in Swiftwater Bill's mine at first. But he quickly became a millionaire by convincing Ottawa politicians and wealthy investors to finance hydraulic dredges to mine 10,000 hectares on a 13-km river frontage.

Yukon Field Force
Policing the flood of new arrivals at Dawson City was almost impossible. To aid the Mounties, the Canadian government created the Yukon Field Force. It was a force of 200 permanent army militiamen who were assigned between 1898 and 1900 to help safeguard the citizens, the banks, and the shipments of gold.

Route to the Yukon
Most travel to the Yukon was by ship to Skagway, Alaska, then by land to the Yukon. In 1897, Inspector J.D. Moodie was ordered to find an overland route through Canada to the Yukon. On September 4, 1897, Moodie and Constable F.J. Fitzgerald began a 14-month trip through the wilderness from Edmonton via the Peace River to the Yukon. After the 2575-km trip, Moodie reported that an overland route was not practical. Access to the Yukon continued via Skagway.

Soapy Smith and Zac Wood

Skagway, Alaska, was a lawless, violent town controlled by an infamous gangster known as "Soapy" Smith. Gang fights, shootings, robberies, and murders were common events. Inspector Zachary Taylor Wood was the great-grandson of Zachary Taylor, the 12th president of the United States. He arrived in Skagway with a force of Mounties, provisions, sled-dog drivers, and 100 sled dogs. Zac Wood set up a NWMP office in Skagway.

When the gold rush of the Trail of '98 was over, fewer than 300 Mounties had aided more than 30,000 new arrivals, inspected 1,360,000 kg of food, and collected $150,000 of gold in custom duties and other fees. Zac Wood had the responsibility of transporting the heavy gold in police kit bags back to Victoria on the CPR steamer *Tarter*.

With his men, disguised as boatmen, carrying the baggage, Zac approached the ship, but his path was blocked by Soapy Smith and his gang. The captain of the *Tarter* had sailors armed with rifles on deck, covering the crowded dockyard. Soapy's hoodlums began to push and shove Zac and his men. As Soapy and Zac stood nose to nose, violence seemed unavoidable. Zac stood his ground; Soapy backed off. The baggage of gold was saved. A month after the incident, Soapy was killed by a vigilante from Skagway's new citizen's committee.

End of the Gold Rush

Most of the miners and merchants who flocked to the Yukon expecting instant wealth were disappointed and disillusioned. Instead of gold, they encountered discomfort, injuries, starvation, disease, and death. The majority departed as quickly, and as penniless, as they had arrived. But thanks to the firm control of the Mounties, they were safe from thieves and outlaws.

The Yukon Territory was created on June 13, 1898. In 1898, the population of Dawson City was 30,000, but in a few fast years, the gold rush was over. Within four years, the population was only 1000, and by 1910, Dawson City had become a ghost town.

Arctic Patrols

The tension and turmoil caused by the gold rush in the Yukon eclipsed another northern duty assigned to the NWMP. It had the formidable challenge of policing Canada's rugged subarctic. Hundreds of Arctic patrols were completed by the Mounties. Valiant officers travelled thousands of kilometres by foot and dogsled, depending on hunting, fishing, and caches of hidden food for survival. They slept in igloos or primitive shelters.

In 1890, the NWMP sent a patrol to York Factory on Hudson Bay. By 1893, the Mounties had arrived in the Athabasca wilderness. In 1897, Inspector A.M. "Buzz" Jarvis reached Fort Resolution on Great Slave Lake. New detachments were created at Fort Chipewyan, Athabasca Landing, and Lesser Slave Lake. Police authority expanded to the Arctic Ocean.

In 1903, a dispute between Canada and the U.S. over the Alaska boundary line was won by the Americans. Canada realized it had to protect its territories from U.S. whalers on the Arctic coast. To decide if Canada needed Arctic police posts, Superintendent Constantine journeyed to Fort McPherson. He left Sergeant F.J. Fitzgerald in the area for the winter.

Hearing that American whalers were supplying illegal alcohol to the local Inuit, Fitzgerald travelled to Herschel Island to spend the winter in a sod house. He halted the liquor trading, and by 1905, N Division had been formed with its headquarters at Athabasca Landing.

From Halifax, a detachment of 16 Mounties sailed to Fullerton in 1903 on the S.S. *Neptune*. It was led by Superintendent J.D. Moodie, who by 1904 was in charge of M Division, which protected the Hudson Bay region. Fullerton's return mail patrol to Churchill was a 1770-km trip.

The Mounties of N and M Divisions used winter dogsled patrols. In late December 1904, Constable H.G. Mapley set out on a mail patrol from Dawson, found a shortcut through the mountains, and arrived at Fort McPherson after travelling 765 km in about a month.

In June 1908, a young French Canadian, Inspector E.A. Pelletier, was ordered to discover a route between N and M divisions. His small party of explorers started from Athabasca. They battled swarms of insects and the rough terrain on the long, perilous trip. Hauling heavy supplies over dozens of portages, the group arrived at Chesterfield Inlet by August. In the winter, Pelletier completed the second part of the trek by dogsled, going south to Churchill, Norway House, and Gimli. The patrol travelled 4830 km. By 1919, 70 Mounties in 25 detachments were protecting the Arctic.

NORTHERN CANADA

Route of *St. Roch*

East 1940-42 ————————

West 1944 ------------

ALASKA

BEAUFORT SEA

GREENLAND

BAFFIN BAY

BANKS IS.

Herschel Is.

VICTORIA ISLAND

BAFFIN ISLAND

Fort MacPherson

Coppermine

NORTHWEST TERRITORIES

YUKON

Yellowknife

Fort Laird

Chesterfield Inlet

Fort Nelson

HUDSONS BAY

65

Arctic Mounties and Inuit Outlaws

A famous Arctic Mountie was Inspector C.D. "Denny" LaNauze. In 1915, he went in search of two Inuit men, Sinnisiak and Uluksak, who had robbed and murdered two priests. Denny LaNauze was aided by Corporal W.V. Bruce, who followed one of the killers to the remote Victoria Island, where no Mountie had been before. There Corporal Bruce arrested the culprit Sinnisiak. A week later, Denny LaNauze apprehended Uluksak on an island in the Coronation Gulf. The two Mounties and their prisoners travelled to the isolated Herschel Island aboard the *Alaska*, a ship with the Canadian Arctic Expedition. From that remote outpost, they began a three-month trip to Edmonton. The killers were found guilty, but their death sentences were commuted to life imprisonment. The Inuit were returned to the Arctic to serve their time as prisoners of the Mounties, rather than in a penitentiary. The two Inuit worked for the police for a few years, but then were permitted to return to their own people.

Another legendary Arctic Mountie was Inspector F.H. French, the nephew of the force's first commissioner. In 1916, he led the search for three Inuit from Bathurst Inlet. They had killed two explorers named Radford and Street. Travelling by foot and dogsleds pulled by 25 huskies, French and Sergeant-Major T.B. Caulkin began a patrol that took 10 months to journey 8245 km. Frequently on the edge of starvation, they had to kill some of their dogs in order to feed the surviving animals. They became lost in the barren Arctic, survived blizzards, and constructed igloo shelters. They suffered from snow-blindness for three agonizing weeks. The investigation concluded that the Inuit had been provoked, and were blameless in the deaths of the explorers.

Lost in the Arctic

On December 21, 1910, the experienced Inspector Francis Joseph Fitzgerald led a routine patrol of four dog teams, which set out from Fort McPherson for the 736-km trip to Dawson City. With him were Constables Richard Taylor and George Kinney, as well as Special Constable Sam Carter. In the deceptive Arctic, the patrol took a wrong turn. The temperature dropped to 62 degrees below zero, and the winds were wicked. The lost patrol ran out of food. The frozen remains of the Mounties were discovered on March 12, 1911. They had starved to death.

Panning for Gold

The Klondike prospector's pan was his or her most important tool. Using it requires skill and practice.

What you need:
- magnet
- small shovel
- metal pan 22 to 30 cm in diameter
- small stream or creek bed with a sandy bottom

What to do:

1. Scoop some sand from the bottom of a stream or creek, enough to fill half the pan.
2. Dip the pan in water to cover the sand. Stir the mixture.
3. Using both hands, tilt the pan slightly away from you. Slosh the mixture in a circular motion to separate the light particles of earth out and over the rim of the pan.
4. Pieces of gold and iron pyrite, heavy sand, small lumps of clay, and gravel will remain in the sand. Examine these and remove them by hand.
5. Using clear water, repeat the process.
6. If the remaining sand is magnetic, it can be removed with a magnet.
7. The remaining metallic specs in the pan may be gold dust or pyrite. The pyrite will be a light yellow. If there is gold, it will be a rich orange colour. Good luck!

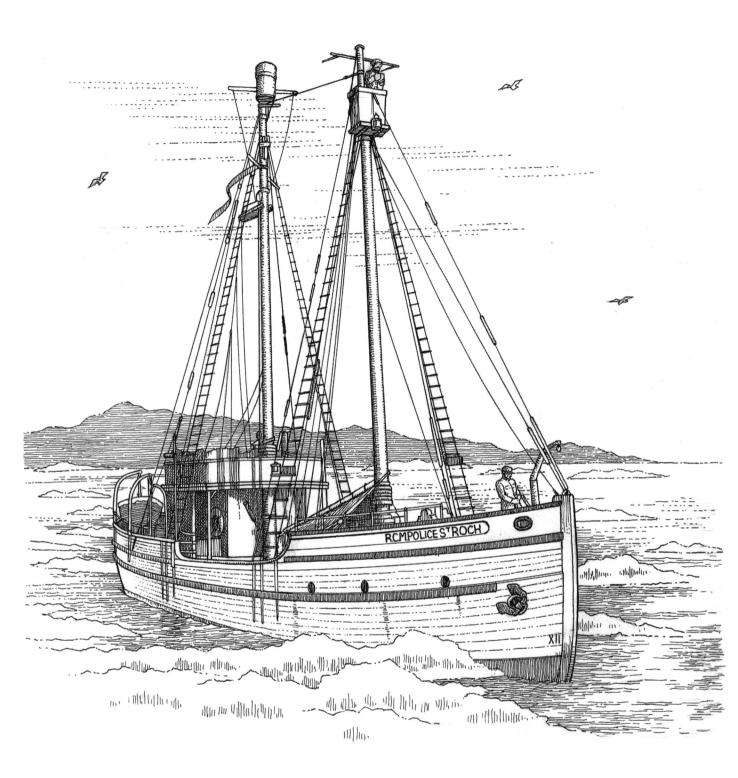

CHAPTER **6** *The RCMP*

Henry Larson, Robin Cameron, Bev Busson, and Others

By the end of the 19th century, the legendary stories about the bravery and achievements of the NWMP had become famous throughout the world.

In 1897, a detachment of Mounties represented Canada at Queen Victoria's Diamond Jubilee in London, England. The Mounties also participated in the ceremonies when Edward VII was crowned king in 1901 and George V in 1910.

Changing Names

The original Mounted Police Force of the North-West Territories was renamed the North-West Mounted Police (NWMP) in 1879. From 1904 to 1920, it was known as the Royal North-West Mounted Police (RNWMP). The "Royal" was an honour awarded by King Edward VII for the Mounties' military service during the Boer War (1899-1902) in South Africa. The RNWMP became the Royal Canadian Mounted Police (RCMP) in 1920 when it absorbed the Dominion Police force in eastern Canada.

The Great War

During the Great War (1914-1918), the government kept the Mounties home to protect Canada from possible internal sabotage. Sam Steele, at age 66, became an army general. He raised and trained the Canadian 2nd Division and took it to England. In 1918, the RNWMP was permitted to send two cavalry squadrons to the war in Europe.

71

Government Fears and Labour Strikes

In 1919, the government feared that labour unrest could spread in Canada. It ordered the RNWMP to suppress the massive Winnipeg General Strike organized by labour unions. On Bloody Saturday, June 21, the Mounties fired into a mob of thousands of strikers, killing one and wounding 30.

In 1929, the Great Depression began, fuelling poverty and protest. On government orders, the RCMP confronted union demonstrators. In Estevan, Saskatchewan, in 1931, three striking coal miners were killed in a confrontation with the Mounties. In 1935, the RCMP was commanded to stop a protest march from Regina to Ottawa. It incited the Regina Riot; one police officer and one rioter were killed.

RCMP Boats and Ships

Canoes and small boats were important vessels for the early Mounties who had to navigate Canada's endless forest rivers, mountain streams, and prairie lakes. In 1890, the NWMP obtained a sailing ship called *Keewartin* to patrol Lake Winnipeg. Within months, it sank in a severe storm. Two crew members died. Steam-powered boats were used on the Yukon River.

The *St. Roch*

In 1928, the *St. Roch* was built for the RCMP to patrol the Arctic Ocean. Its captain, Sergeant Henry A. Larson, left Vancouver on June 23, 1940, navigated the icy Arctic waters, and arrived in Halifax on October 11, 1942. It was the first ship to travel through the frozen Northwest Passage from the Pacific Ocean to the Atlantic Ocean. Then it turned around and made the 11,323-km trip back in only 86 days. The *St. Roch* became the first ship to circumnavigate the North American continent in 1950 when it sailed again to Halifax via the Panama canal. In 1954, it was retired from service.

Searching for Smugglers

In 1932, the RCMP Marine Section was created. It had 35 ships that were used to capture smugglers on the east and west coasts, as well as in the Gulf of St. Lawrence. In World War II, it became part of the Canadian navy for the war years. After 1945, the Marine Section returned to the RCMP.

RCMP Patrol Vessels (PVs)

By 2007, five RCMP patrol vessels (PVs), with computer and electronic navigation equipment and radar, were protecting the east and west coasts of Canada. These fast patrol catamarans are powered by twin 820-horsepower D2840 LE401 V-10 Man diesel engines and have a top speed of 36 knots. At other locations, there are 377 smaller RCMP boats less than 9.2 m long.

New Technologies

Since the 1920s, the RCMP has expanded and modernized. It utilizes fingerprinting, a crime index, a firearms registration, a photo section, and a forensic laboratory. Dr. Frances McGill worked in medical science, forensic medicine and pathology as director of the Saskatchewan RCMP laboratory from 1922 to 1942. She has been dubbed the "First Woman Mountie."

Mountie Spies

By the 1920s, the Mounties were in the business of spying. They were responsible for counter-intelligence and national security. In 1950, the Special Branch of the RCMP was created. In 1962, the Directorate of Security and Intelligence was formed, and in 1970, the RCMP Security Service was established. By 1972, the Canadian Police Information Centre was operating. During the 1970s, the Mounties assumed responsibility for airport security, VIP security, drug enforcement, and economic crime.

Mountie Dogs

Frontier Mounties used their own dogs to track criminals. Dogsleds pulled by huskies were important for transportation in the Arctic. The RCMP dog section was established in 1935, with three German shepherds named Black Lux, Dale of Cawsalta, and Sultan. The RCMP Police Dog Service Training Centre was created at Innisfail, Alberta, in 1965. The dogs are purebred German or Belgium shepherds (Malinois). Fewer than 20 percent of the dogs that begin training are chosen to serve with the RCMP.

Duties of a Mountie Dog	Facts about a Mountie Dog
• locating lost people • tracking criminals • searching for narcotics/explosives • VIP protection • crowd control • hostage rescue • avalanche search and rescue	• dog and handler are a team • cost to train a dog team is $60,000 • cost to maintain a dog is $1000/year • over 100 dog teams in Canada • a dog can search a car in 3 minutes • a dog can work for 4 hours • a dog retires after 7 years of service

Walt Disney and the Mounties

The last dogsled patrol on March 11, 1969, used two teams of Siberian Huskies. They were the descendants of 34 sleigh dogs that Walt Disney donated to the force after filming the movie *Nikki: Wild Dog of the North*.

The media, producers of merchandise, and many others have created numerous Mountie paraphernalia and products. Often they mock or insult the Mountie image. In 1995 the Mounted Police Foundation was set up to protect the RCMP image. It had no expertise in copyright, licensing or marketing, so it contracted those responsibilities to the Walt Disney Co. Ltd. (Canada). Canadians disapproved of the Mountie image being regulated by Walt Disney. When the contract expired in 2000, it was not renewed.

74

Musical Ride

In the frontier days, NWMP officers devised the first musical rides as a source of entertainment for themselves and the local communities. They displayed their skills at horseback riding by performing a series of movements based on cavalry drill manoeuvres.

Today the Musical Ride consists of a troop of 32 riders and horses. The riders are regular police officers who are assigned to the ride for three years. Each year one-third of the participants rotate back to police duties as a new crop of officers, with at least two years on the force, are trained at Rockcliffe, Ontario, where the Musical Ride is based.

Mad Trapper of Rat River

On December 26, 1931, Constable A.W. King went to the isolated cabin of a Yukon trapper on Rat River because local Native people had complained that he was stealing from their traplines. The man refused to open the door. When King returned on December 31 with Constable R.G. McDowell, King was shot in the chest, and had to be rushed to hospital by dogsled. The dangerous gunman became a media star as newspapers and radio broadcasters spread the story of the "Mad Trapper of Rat River."

On January 10, 1932, a patrol of Mounties and volunteers returned with flares and dynamite. Despite a 15-hour gun battle and dynamite blasts against the cabin walls, they could not force the trapper from his fortress. When a third Mountie patrol arrived on January 19, the cabin was empty. A fourth patrol discovered him in another barricade on January 30, but during the clash, Constable E. Millan was killed.

The RCMP employed Captain "Wop" May, a bush pilot who had been a WWI Flying Ace, to fly Constable W.S. Carter with tear bombs and more ammunition to the isolated Aklavik location. For the next two weeks as the world watched and listened, the famous pilot made many trips from Aklavik to the posse tracking the fugitive. On February 17, the posse caught up with the desperado and killed him with a blaze of bullets. Staff Sergeant E.F. Hersey, a volunteer from the Canadian army, led the attack. He was wounded in his knee, elbow, and chest. Wop May saved his life by flying him to the Aklavik hospital.

The true identity of the Mad Trapper, and the reason for his desperate fear of being captured, were never discovered. The incident made it clear that the RCMP needed to have its own airplanes.

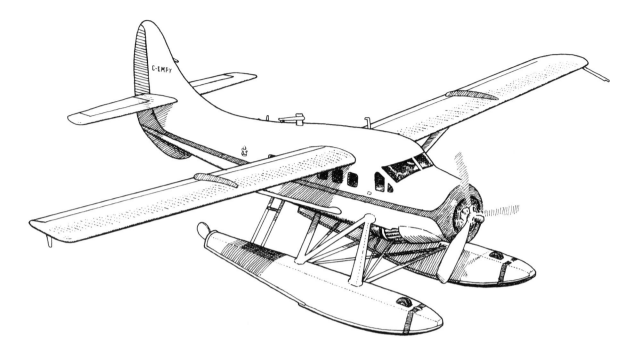

Prohibition and Rum-Runners

From 1920 to 1933, the United States introduced Prohibition, which made the brewing, sale, and transportation of alcohol illegal. Since Canada had no prohibition laws against alcohol, a new black-market industry developed. Criminals known as rum-runners illegally smuggled alcohol into the U.S. In 1932, the RCMP were given air force planes to stop rum-runners.

Dragonflies, a Goose, and Helicopters

By 1937, the RCMP had realized that airplanes were necessary for law enforcement, and the RCMP Air Services was created. It purchased four Dragonflies and a Norseman. In 1945, the Mounties acquired more planes including a Grumman Goose, which served for 49 years. In 1971, the first helicopter was added to the fleet. By 2007, the Air Services had 41 aircraft.

Military Police
From 1939 to 1945, the RCMP participated in World War II. The Mounties were responsible for national security at home, and the No. 1 Provost Company was created as military police overseas.

Bank Robbery Bravery (April 3, 1956)
In Maillardville, British Columbia, Constable H.M.C. Johnstone responded to a bank alarm and encountered three armed men. When he entered the bank, one robber shot him. As he lay wounded, a second burglar began blasting at him. Johnstone returned fire. The third thief ran past him out the door, shooting point-blank at the fallen Mountie. Johnstone, riddled with bullet wounds in his finger, hand, shoulder, hip, forearm, side, and chest, staggered to his feet, pursued two of the bandits outside, but dropped in the street. Johnstone had wounded both assailants inside the bank. They also fell to the ground, one wounded, the other dead. The officer sat up, pointing his empty gun at the third robber who instantly surrendered. Johnstone was the first Mountie to receive the George Medal for "acts of great bravery."*

Separatists and Scandals
In the 1960s, a Marxist terrorist group, the Front de libération du Québec (FLQ), was formed to support an independent Quebec, separate from Canada. The saboteurs set off over 200 bombs, killing at least five people. During the October Crisis of 1970, terrorist cells kidnapped James Cross, a British diplomat, who was freed after 60 days of negotiations. The kidnappers were deported to Cuba. Pierre Laporte, a Quebec cabinet minister, was also kidnapped. He was murdered by his abductors. To deal with the crisis, Prime Minister Pierre Elliott Trudeau enacted the War Measures Act, using the army to protect government offices and officials from the terrorists.

* The George Medal was established by King George VI in September 1940.

There were 947 suspects arrested; 62 were charged.

In a scandalous aftermath, the RCMP were accused of subversive defence activities. In 1981, a Commission of Inquiry recommended that the RCMP Security Service be replaced by a new intelligence agency, the Canadian Security Intelligence Service (CSIS).

New Mounties, New Rules
- 1974: The RCMP changed the physical description and height requirements to allow women and ethnic minorities to qualify as Mountie recruits.
- 1975: Troop 17 was the first group of female Mountie recruits to begin training at Regina in September 1974. They graduated on March 3, 1975.
- 1990: Baltej Singh Dhillon was the first Sikh Mountie to wear a turban in place of the stetson. The force changed its uniform rules to allow turbans.
- 2001: After the terrorist attack on the twin towers in New York City on September 11, 2001, politicians placed the RCMP back in the spy role, responsible for internal security.
- 2006: The first public same-sex marriage between two Mounties, Constables Jason Tree and David Connors, took place in Nova Scotia.

Tragedy in Alberta
James Roszko, a 46-year-old violent loner in Rochfort Bridge, Alberta, had been in trouble since he was a teenager. His love of guns and hatred of police were known to the RCMP at the nearby Mayerthorpe detachment.

On March 3, 2005, four Mounties arrived at Roszko's farm to recover stolen car parts. They discovered a marijuana grow operation. Constables Tony Gordon (age 28), Brock Myrol (age 29), Leo Johnston (age 32), and Peter Schiemann (age 25), encountered a deadly surprise. All were shot to death. When a tactical unit stormed the property, Roszko killed himself.*

* In July 2007, two other men, Dennis Cheeseman, 23, and Shawn Hennesey, 28, were charged with first-degree murder for being involved with the crime.

RCMP Honour Roll

With the honour of wearing the red tunic comes the danger of dying. On March 15, 1989, Constable Della S. Beyak, age 21, was responding to an accident in a blinding snowstorm. She struck another car head on and died. On December 9, 1989, Sub-Constable Nancy Puttkemery of the Air Services in Calgary was also a victim of poor visibility in heavy snow. Her airplane struck a guy wire of a radio tower. The Cessna 182 crashed, instantly killing Nancy and Sub-Constable Vincent Timms. In 2006, Constables Robin Cameron and Marc Bourdages, while investigating a domestic dispute in Saskatchewan, were shot to death by 41-year-old Curtis Dagenais. The entire RCMP Honour Roll is in libraries and on the Internet.

Commissioner Resigns

In 2006, political pressure forced Commissioner Giuliano Zaccardelli to resign as the head of the RCMP after the FBI in the U.S. arrested Maher Arar, a Syrian-Canadian with a dual citizenship. The RCMP was accused of giving improper information about Mr. Arar to American authorities, who sent him to his native Syria where he was tortured as a terrorist suspect.

Eventually, the Canadian government secured Maher's release, and he returned to Canada. Mr. Arar received an apology from Prime Minister Stephen Harper and $12 million in compensation. U.S. officials continued to list him as a person to be detained if found in the U.S.

First Female Commissioner

On December 16, 2006, following the resignation of Giuliano Zaccardelli, Bev Busson became the 21st commissioner of the RCMP. Bev had been one of the first women to graduate as a Mountie in 1975. Throughout her career, she was awarded many honours and medals.

The RCMP Today

Today more than 16,000 RCMP officers guard and protect 200 Canadian cities and towns. They act as the provincial police force in eight provinces and three territories. Only the provinces of Ontario and Quebec have their own provincial police forces.

RCMP Regional Divisions

Atlantic Region

Newfoundland: B Division
Prince Edward Island: L Division
Nova Scotia: H Division (Region Headquarters)
New Brunswick: J Division

Central Region

Ottawa, Ontario: A Division (National Headquarters) *
Quebec: C Division
Ontario: O Division

Northwest Region

Manitoba: D Division
Saskatchewan: F Division (Region Headquarters) **
Northwest Territories: G Division
Alberta: K Division
Nunavut: V Division

Pacific Region

British Columbia: E Division (Region Headquarters)
Yukon: M Division

* Canadian Police College is in Ottawa.
** Training Academy and RCMP Heritage Centre are in Regina.

RCMP Ranks and Numbers

Commissioned Ranks		Non-Commissioned Ranks	
Commissioner	1	Corps Sergeant Major	1
Deputy Commissioners	8	Sergeant Majors	6
Assistant Commissioners	26	Staff Sergeant Majors	11
Chief Superintendents	58	Staff Sergeants	791
Superintendents	162	Sergeants	1,726
Inspectors	382	Corporals	3,098
		Constables	10,705

Civilian Members

In 2007, there were 7604 RCMP employees who did not have police powers. They have technical, scientific, computer, and administrative duties. RCMP statistics are updated yearly at http://www.rcmp.ca/factsheets/index_e.htm

International Police Role

The Mounties are known and respected throughout the world. The International Operations is responsible for the RCMP Liaison Officer Program, which provides person-to-person linkages with foreign police to assist with major international criminal investigations.

The Mounties frequently assist and train police officers in other countries. Since 1989, the International Peace Operations of the RCMP has performed international police roles in Namibia, Yugoslavia, Haiti, South Africa, Rwanda, Kosovo, Bosnia, Central African Republic, Sierra Leone, East Timor, Guatemala, Croatia, Western Sahara, the Netherlands, The Hague, Iraq, Jordan, Côte-d'Ivoire, Congo, and Afghanistan.

Interpol Ottawa is the National Central Bureau for Interpol and Europol. It coordinates information exchange with foreign police forces throughout the world.

First Non-Cop Commissioner

In 2007, other scandals emerged involving the terrorist bombing of the Air India flight in 1985, misuse of funds in the RCMP Pension Plan, and complaints from RCMP officers of bad management of the force. In July 2007, William Elliott, who had never been a member of any police force, was appointed the new RCMP commissioner. His assignment was to command and reform the force.

RCMP Heritage Centre

In May 2007, the awe-inspiring RCMP Heritage Centre opened on the historic grounds of the RCMP Academy in Regina. It features modern state-of-the-art exhibits and interactive multimedia technology.

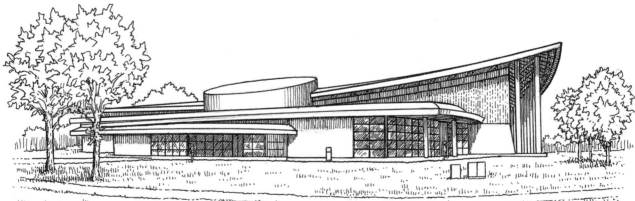

Fingerprinting and Identification

Each individual's fingerprints are unique. Police can identify suspects whose fingerprints have been found at the scene of a crime.

What you need:
- a rubber roller
- water-based ink
- magnifying glass
- a sheet of glass or hard plastic
- 10 pieces of smooth paper

What to do:
1. Cut out 8 cm x 12 cm pieces of paper, at least 10 pieces.
2. Roll out a small area of ink until it forms a thin film on the glass.

Original size

Magnified 3X

3. Lightly roll a friend's thumb in the ink.
4. Carefully roll the inked thumb on a piece of paper. Repeat this on a second piece of paper. Write the person's name or "alias" on the back of one sheet. Lay the sheet without a name aside.
5. Repeat the process with other friends until you have a file of five or six individual thumbprints.
6. Now turn the blank sheets face down on a table. Shuffle them around.
7. Select at random one of the blank sheets and turn it over to the print side. Now go to your "collected file."
8. Using the magnifying glass, compare the subject's print to those in your file until you can identify it.

The more prints you have on file, the more challenging the process will become. The Mounties and other police agencies have millions of fingerprints on file.

Mountie Crossword Puzzle

ACROSS

3. Mountie who died when his Arctic patrol was lost in the winter of 1910-1911.
5. His nickname was Bear Child.
6. Legendary Mountie in the Arctic.
7. Government agent massacred with seven settlers at Frog Lake.
9. Rank of the commanding officer of the RCMP.
13. Mountie, known as Bull's Head, who befriended the Blackfoot chiefs.
15. Blood warrior who murdered Sergeant William Wilde in 1896.
16. Famous Yukon city known as the Paris of the North.
18. The Mountie who gained the trust of Sitting Bull.
20. Métis rebel leader known as the Prince of the Plains.
21. Mountie who stood up to a gangster named "Soapy" Smith.
22. Cree rebel chief who defeated the army and the Mounties at Cut Knife Hill.
23. Mountie who faced down a mob of railway rioters at Beaver Crossing in 1885.
25. Mountie superintendent whose force was ambushed by rebels at Duck Lake in 1885.
26. First Mountie to be murdered.
28. First female RCMP commissioner.
31. Gold was discovered here in 1896.
33. Prairie rebels were defeated at this battle in 1885.
34. Group of people who led the rebellion in 1885.
35. Name given to the Mounties in 1920.

DOWN

1. _____ Kate, nickname of Special Constable Kate Ryan, one of the first women on the force in 1898.
2. Famous Mountie who protected the railway line and gold miners.
4. Undercover agent sent to investigate the Hardwick Gang.
8. Mountie inspector who abandoned Fort Pitt to Cree rebels.
9. Female Mountie who was killed along with her partner in 2006.
10. Prime minister who created the NWMP.
11. Location of the RCMP Heritage Centre.
12. Captain of the Mountie ship that was first to circumnavigate North America.
14. First Mountie to wear a turban.
15. Blackfoot chief who signed Treaty No. 7.
17. Mountie who convinced Chief Piapot to leave the CPR lands.
19. American train robber whose gang was captured by the Mounties in 1906.
23. First Mountie commissioner who led the trek west to the Sweet Grass Hills.
24. Leader of the 1885 rebellion who was executed for high treason.
27. Canadian gold miner who became a millionaire by using hydraulic dredges.
29. Female gold miner known as the First Lady of the Yukon.
30. Native people who arrived in Canada after massacring General Custer's cavalry.
32. Name given to the Mounties in 1879.

Across
- 3. FITZGERALD
- 5. POTTS
- 6. LANAUZE
- 7. QUINN
- 9. COMMISSIONER
- 13. MACLEOD
- 15. CHARCOAL
- 16. DAWSON
- 18. WALSH
- 20. DUMONT
- 22. POUNDMAKER
- 23. FURY
- 25. CROZIER
- 26. GRABURN
- 28. BUSSON
- 31. YUKON
- 33. BATOCHE
- 34. MÉTIS
- 35. RCMP

Down
- 1. KOD…
- 2. STEELE
- 4. IRVINE
- 8. DICKENS
- 10. MACDONALD
- 11. REGINA
- 12. LARSON
- 14. DHILLON
- 15. CROWFOOT
- 17. WILDE
- 19. MI…
- 21. WHOOPUP
- 23. FRENCH
- 24. RIEL
- 27. BOO…
- 29. BLACK
- 30. SIOUX
- 32. NWMP

Index